Odd Beauty,
Strange Fruit

Odd Beauty, Strange Fruit

Susan Swartwout

Brick Mantel Books
Bloomington, Indiana

Published by Brick Mantel Books, USA

Brick Mantel
BOOKS

www.BrickMantelBooks.com
info@BrickMantelBooks.com
An imprint of Pen & Publish, Inc.
Bloomington, Indiana
(314) 827-6567
www.PenandPublish.com

Print ISBN: 978-1-941799-05-5
eBook ISBN: 978-1-941799-06-2

Cover Design: Jennifer Geist

Always for Jonathan

"When you're born, you get a ticket to the freak show."
—George Carlin

Table of Contents

Tenderest

Southeastern Atlanta Fair, 1962

When our eyes have opened to shadows in mote-thick air of the circus tent,
when old men's droning of what circus once was and mothers' sibilant *: hissing*
scolding to restless children has slowed to a barely perceptible pulse,

the carney throws back the bedsheet curtain, strides to stage's edge
where he pauses, above us. In the growled breath of a crank caller, he twangs
his whiskey-hard speil: *what you are about to see . . . nothin' ever like it*

on earth . . . tenderest part of the body . . . beyond human understandin' . . . Electra.
From behind the bedsheet shuffles a scrawny woman whose bones knuckle
creped skin, her face the lined mask of a thousand farm wives: she reveals

no opinion. The carney's arms and yellowed grin refer to her widely: door
number three: his prize in the faded two-piece swimsuit, Marilyn of canvas
roadshows. She stands mute, like the woman in Anderson's tale who feeds

and feeds the world until she dies in moonlight, reborn a romantic
instant in villagers' eyes as a lovely girl—mistaken and taken for what
she never was. We sit silent, praying for transformation to save her from us.

The carney reveals a cattle prod and the timepiece that is our breathing halts.
He waves the rod like a flag: it sings, whines to be fed—she is hypnotized.
The tenderest part of the human body, says the carney. He slides the rod,

horizontal, in front of her, not touching. Our nerves become her. Before her
breasts, then level with pelvis, he pauses the rod *the tenderest part* and moves
upward as if he would stroke her—for us—as if he would enter her on stage.

Rod at her throat, her tongue takes its cue, appears automatically in a curve
as if taking a bow *the tenderest* and he lays it down: rod onto flesh. The fake
smoke of his hell and susurration of his pardon that keeps her tied to this place
rise over her head like a benediction, resigning all faith in the tenderest part.

Five Deceits of the Hand

1.

While your hair is still silk of young corn,
your baby teeth tiny kernels, you learn to count,
to take stock of things around you. Numbers
come like promises, dreams for the tallying.
You sign for them with your infant fingers,
copied from the silver side of your parents' looking
glass: Put your fingers like this. That's One, and the sky
you point to is enclosed. This *one* you hold in front
of your face, the shield between you and your teacher
who thrusts the dream of having upon you. Two
is a scout promise that will challenge your quests,
and three, fingers a trident after you overpower outsiders,
two digits who bow into your palm. Four, your hand
salutes the mirror; Good. Five is a show of no weapons,
until you learn to hide them behind your body, behind
the trick of openness. Two hands double your grasp.

2.

The diminishing of all earthlings
fills you: cornfields stripped of green
and gold flesh, trees lowered to mulch,
a bird skeleton alone in the garden.
Friends vanish like misplaced directions
into skies you used to claim. Age begins
sucking your bones until you lean shriveled
 into the mouth of harvest.
            Your fingers cannot name this;
            you sign for the pain, folding
memories into your pocket like the photos
of unlined faces that stare from your wallet.
Dreams drift into the pending of numbered days.
At a cloud's edge you find the touch of loss
counts you no different than all earthlings,
where body slips away.

First Fight

Louisianan up north, I still smell delta mud: first
grade classroom windows opened out like beetle wings.

Playground sparkled like sequins from the busted glass.
High school boys drank and laid bad girls in the ditch

at the edge. I saw my first cat fight at Jefferson Parish
Elementary. Both girls wore brown oxfords, round skirts

with big slips that frothed when they kicked, and all they did
was kick each other, eerie horses. You could see

their pastel panties; you could almost read the needled day.
Rough boys snickered into fists, hollered, "Git 'er down."

Later that fall I was stabbed in the leg with a yellow pencil,
lil' ol' boy poised like The Thinker outside his classroom.

Dr. Strangelove
for my father

Mother told me what you did
to learn your craft:
corpse wrapped in swaddling cloths
soaked in formaldehyde, the stink
of science that rose from beneath
your double bed. How strange
the coupling of you and my mother,
swift pleasures of the living,
above the tough hide
of preserved carcass, the warm
funky smell of sex untempered
by chemistry's bitter edge.

Thousands of interns
through thousands of years,
thin-lipped, starved for the taste
of their shingles, hide cadavers
in closets, under beds, cover death's
common scents with "Country Fresh
Flowers" or "Ocean Breezes" sprayed
liberally, *PRN.* They return
to their homes to expose thousands
of hard bodies to fluorescent's
calculating glare, track blue vein's
paths, deep purple globes—
cavity's cornucopia—gleaned
from their Frankenstein's monster,
an imago of those still-lifes they'll steal
from necessary death, from flatline's
quakeless fault.   Father,

you called me your term paper,
conceived in a frenzy between classes
and rounds. Decades later, the dead
long dead in a place where pieces
no longer matter. You and I remain
distant nodes in a network of cross-
country kin. Yet I see your face on occasion,
Picassoed in my corner-eyed glance at a mirror.

My image fragments into your eyebrows,
thick hair, sienna eyes, seconds before
I piece myself together again
as a soft-cover text: your version
of the human short story,
written in bed above the dead.

Louisiana Ladies' Watermelon Tea—1890

This photo holds more than pose, cheating
the sepia tone's formal stare, or the proper places
and laces that display these unwed female forms

like iced cakes. The ladies have shared pieces
of themselves the camera will never know,
its gaping eye swallowing the scene like a melon seed,

black seeds the ladies squeeze out
between their lips, preening their images in the spit-
wet surfaces. Three maidens seated on the floor

smile the secret that floats between them
like a mimosa blossom. Their chins are tucked in,
eyes half-mooned under lids that seem to smirk

pure pleasure. One cozies her cheek against the thigh
of a beauty who sits in a parlor chair romancing
the camera, bouquet of ferns tucked into her bodice

by one of the others. Beauty raises her melon slice
to the camera: *Hey ya'll, I've passed on, but you can still see
I'm divine.* She widens her eyes so you can admire

the image of belles, their arched skirts ringing
in memory. Myths of manhunting,
manipulation, are forgiven in their balm of drawl.

The lady who serves the treat invests everything
in her wrists. Plain and tall, she blunts the violence
of a broad-blade knife thrust half-way to hilt

in melon by the subtle swan's neck curve
of her hand into wrist. Her other arm bends
near her waist, the hand swooning backward, falling

into curled fingers and pale iron palm. Center-
poised, she pretends in pose to defer to her friend
who stocks more satin fringe than Maison Blanche.

They glance at each other and smile, yes, sugar.
Keeping these ladies from sweet fruit's excess
has never been simple. Kudzu layers their menfolks' eyes.

Even clocks can't hold us apart from their parlor.
Do call again tomorrow; nothing will change.
The ladies will be here, their fingers sticky with boredom.

The Goddess Discord Brings Her New Doll Buggy into My Yard to Show Off, When I Don't Want Her There

Sonnet a deux

We're born into our language, I've been told;
words, pungent as over-ripened fruit, fall
from baby lips like apples from a gold
ancestery. The classic story recalls
past perfect fruit from angry Discord's hand
marked "For the fairest," meaning instant war
of words, for words, that parsed an ancient land—
just as my five-year-old words went too far
when Discord strolled into my own backyard.
None of us liked her. She wasn't allowed.
She tromped our disdain with her disregard
for "lower class," so I hollered out, loud,
to that neighbor girl, from my lingual niche:
"You yellow-bellied, lily-livered bitch":

old Southern terms I'd heard somewhere like home.
They bounced off nearby dad like a nightmare
echo, words that he didn't want to own
up I'm "born into." Weren't we a grand pair:
me under his arm like a sack of Rome
Beauties, him doing the bad dad goose-step
into the house, his mouth just shy of foam-
ing. Inside, the lecture was only prep;
something about acting like a "lady"
and saying I was sorry to Discord
for my lip, but I deemed it too shady
to be mealy-mouthed to her, the abhorred.
Then his belt swung to strike away words, while
through my tears, I sensed Discord's placid smile.

Strange Fruit

My younger brother was a tough
little dandy, who took any dare:
throw snowballs at cop cars,
swig Mom's perfume,
hula-hula in Dad's boxer shorts,
Dad just down the hall.
So I dared him to enter the fetus
tent, set that week in the grocer's
parking lot, the hot canvas packed
with pickling jars, their floating freaks.
Outside, posters claimed *Frog Baby!* and *Two-
Headed Pony! See Lizerd Boy! Sheep Chile:
Two Hands, Two Hoofs! Gin-yoo-ine!*
I'd pay the nickel , he'd
guess the gimmick, the geek,
the stitches, the ooze that proves
freak is fake, a laugh not a lesson.

A staple in the pony's neck, a thread
at the base of the lizard tail. Yet more
drifts in the jars' gray slough and sog:
Fetal pig in upside-down hell
holds veiled light forever in its eyes.
The sheep child hunches in a frozen
faux fuck, dreams of museums,
country boys. Frogmouthed baby glares
through all we thought we knew,
its lips parted in objection.

                    We never thought
to see paradise parodied in such odd
beauty. Strange fruit best
left where it fell, away from nickel
neverland, floating beyond our ken
and kindness. So
we crept out, silent, to our plain
world of collapse and decay,
mundane replication,
dullwitted DNA.

Sent for the Summer to Mean Texas Granny's Circus

Gateway
Each day gets up like a carney,
Early, hateful as the day's chores
Granny makes me eat
Breakfast: cantaloupe, salted

Attraction 1
Mimosa drapes her backyard like a tent
I hide behind the massive zinnias
They nod, but don't tell
When giant granny-feet slip past

Attraction 2
Can't hide in the brick barbeque pit
She might torchlight my act: behind
Curtain number 3: The Amazing Charbaby

Attraction 3
Don't . . . don'tgo . . . don'tgobackthere
Weeds in the alley taller than a bum
Snakes that scare mean Granny
Granny, look,
This is what I can hold in my hands
Who won't harm me more
Than a boring day

Attraction 4
The Incredible Wasp-Stung Grandkid
Screams the title song to an album
Called "They Came Outta Those Bushes"
Mean Granny out the door like The Green Hornet
Chewing a plug of Redman to spit on the welts

Attraction 5
Phone call to Georgia allowed once a week
Momma, come get me, my lip stuck out
Granny makes chicken noises, fakes
A pout *You're too far into the summer*
Too far to turn back now

The Closing Act
In thirty years, Granny lies speechless
In a hospital bed with Mama brushing her hair
While Granny glares like I'm some stranger. Stubborn
As ever, she will count her minutes until we leave
Then add five more, knowing we're too far away
Then to turn back in time, as she slips away on her own.

Little Brother

The snapshot holds me at ten, leaning
my cheek onto his small head, my
tangled horsetail hair pours over his
natty crew.

He's the good child, soul seared to gleam
by my gasoline temper, kindled envies,
while mother who loves him best polishes
his halo at the table, watches pot roasts
burn dark over their pink torsos.

Daily I count my father's esteem for a dutiful
daughter in good grades, music medals, his
scarce smiles.
                    Little brother joins Cub Scouts
alone, never plays ball or goes fishing, mows
neighborhoods of grass into velvet over and over.

He smiles, photo angel, from under
my smothering hair, hands already folded
over his chest—ten years later he'll try
braking his own heart, a handful of pills
between his words and my understanding
of loss I never imagined.

Our Man Thumb

for Charles S. Stratton: Barnum's "Tom Thumb"

You're our dimpled squash pie, our delight,
      a micro mannikin,
      with a Barnum hairdo
You're a button accordion playing a hopping tune
      the song is nasal
      we will pay anything
You're a bonsai trimmed from your mother's womb
      a one-horned goat
      puffing cigars
You're an ice cube down the back on a hot day
      a wriggle worm
      a brightly striped unknown beetle
You're mother's walking doll that terrifies us
      from the back of the closet
      real teeth, eyes that click open
We probably wouldn't hear you if you walked up
      behind us or slid
      under our beds
You have the moon face of a doting uncle
      with thick fingers
      that probe and pluck
Yardstick length of a man, come down
      from the stage's height
      Let us see
How your mouth's small *o* fits under our feet

Tom Thumb Dreams

He envisions being stowed
under bell-shaped skirts
of red-haired ladies' dresses
at parties. They never reveal
this secret, just sigh.
He dreams an abundance
of women three-feet high.
Or one, please.

In nightmares, he awakens
as an ordinary man
with a nine to five job
in a factory, filthy cap pulled
over bowl-chopped curls,
finds his way home
to a family of strangers
who don't even notice
he enters the room.
He mugs, tap dances
on the kitchen table,
but his feet make no sound.
Dream fractures to day-
break, him screaming:
Look at me, look
what I can do.

He flies in his dreams
higher than anyone,
a tiny wren cresting eagles.
When he soars
he lords over crowds
that nest like any audience:
all flat heads and open
mouths. Begging for it.

Boogie Land

Father forced me to leave when I was sixteen;
his low voice calling from Chicago,
a new house waiting like a cold nest.
A train dragged me sobbing from the South,
black knife cutting through kudzu hills,
laying them to each side like breasts
of warm chickens portioned

by my great-grandmother Simmang,
her coiled brown braid a sign of her love
of symmetry and order—the meat divided,
the pot already bubbling, sage-smell thick as smog
in her kitchen—me, still picking feathers
between my fingers, off my stained shirt.
She selected, I plucked, she cooked,
I cleaned up—the younger female
taking as given the tasks of blood and slop.

A train stole my body from Louisiana.
I awoke to horizons of fields, cut-cornstalks
like the stubble of a strange man's cheek,
boogie land, yellowed and filled with wind
that whipped seedy hair: prairie grasses wild
with disorder under wired fences.

Chicago was gray/black and dark red.
Mother, me, sister, and brothers
in thin cotton coats staggered
from the station tipsy with Loop wind,
stopped in the cold by a drunk
who wanted to carry my blonde baby sister
through filthy snow. My brothers and I
circled her like cows, our eyes stupid
with ignorance of this world, my hands
shooing him as if he were a chicken
from our neighbor Bichon's. But

Mother stood with her face transformed.
Fear opened her, mouth gaping
and silent in front of him;

everything she'd read about rape
and death came home in this one drunk,
her eyes round as fishes',
as if she would lie heavy and still
for a stranger's knife
to cleave her in two,
the awkward obedience of the catch,

like Michelle, a girl in Miss Doubet's
third grade class, who never waited
coming out of Thibadoux Market
ahead of the rest of us buying our wax lips
and fingernails on the way home from school.
She had sashayed a half block ahead
when we stepped into sunlight,
the car door already opening
like a dark mouth, her lips responding.

We stood round-eyed as sheep,
watching, as if in slow motion,
the man's hand clutch her arm,
her white candy bag spill
onto hot pavement, Michelle's
legs fluttering
as the car stole her body,
the scream of its tires
burning in our throats—
learning how a female
in this place mistakes as task
the given of her gracious answer,
how compliance leads her
from virtue's bright blood.

One of the Lesser Gods

Louisiana was hunter's paradise,
and my father was god when I was young
and in love with his graven image: the country
drives, camping by mountain streams, the curious
eyes of beasts he knew by name, pulling silver
fish out of dark water,
                     and then his snake-strike
temper, the stacks of purple-black paintings, *... bruises?*
his need not to hear any new word but to be
the last one. He told me once when he killed

some small creature, he always
gave some of it back to the earth—
the entrails buried; the head, burned.
I know now he gave back what he couldn't
use. The smoke curls over my head,
flaming eyes burn clear of tears, tongue
splits into two question marks
from the heat. They say embers live
long enough to be dangerous. I breathe
through the flames and black water, immersed
in our natures, but planning when I die
to go into the fire whole.

Family History

Be a light unto yourself.
—The Buddha

A grandfather who shot himself,
brother with a gutful of pills,
a father who oilpaints in blacks and blues,
and you with your self-tarnished armor.

Light and shadow envelopes your hand-
me-down layers of confusion—
freedom, just a textbook word
written in an ancestral language.
Images scoured of hope race past
the brain's silvered corridors,
from the chemical soup
stirred for decades by grief-
stained grandparents—
a recipe inked in despair,
a familial chant that drowns out
white noise of occasional joy.

Your burdened brain hatches
nightmare flights; you sleep with all
your windows open to tree branches
that reach out with sympathetic arms,
made strong by sunshine.

Some mornings you want to
disappear, barefoot in your blue
shroud, courage and resignation
seesawing on your shoulders.
These blue-blurred days

make you think you
could walk into the woods and die
quiet, like an animal rather than face
the dark world you have watched
grow around you, grief basting
your brain as the nightmare
called genes brews your fate
in its teacup, wondering if you
can decide whether or not
to stir in the bitter lemon.

Rear Window

In '66, teens weekend workshopped
in Thornton Woods: how to neck,
stage the outline of romantic plays
in the frame of cars' rear windows.
Silhouetted by city lamps, body parts
posed, performed each ancient act.
The park drive squirmed, engorged
with cars, a mile of tree darkness,
asphalt funked with love's
latex detritus detailed by zoo sounds
in groans, howls, hallelujahs.

I babed in the Woods with a guy
I'd just met, compelled by the moth-
to-flame love call duet: sex/status.
He wore leather, smoked, had car
and job. I was jailbait, wore skirts cut
to *here,* tucked my nerves in tight.
When it came to silhouettes,
I said heads; he talked tails.
Like Scheherazade, saving neck,
saving face, I canted Woods rumors:

chewed tires and crazies, bullets
in brains, the guy who went for a piss
and never returned. His girl shook
in the car all night, her heart's
beat-beat echoed *drip-drip* on the hood.
At dawn's first light, she made out
her date's shape, hung from a branch,
blood leaking from cut throat to car.
She never again spoke, tragic fate for a teen.

He smirked, but must have believed
me, believed boogiemen leer, scheme
behind night's veil. We wrestled an hour
in the car in my driveway—locus of nothing
more deadly than indifferent dad—
practiced positions and passion's pretense,
until mother produced her warning, porch lights
flashing off and on, end of act one.

Orpheus in Her Stars: The First Time

1.
Like picking saddle oxfords
she chooses this round-eyed boy
from high school French class,
just as anxious to work up
his own nightmoves. They hold hands
in the film-dark, ignore
subtitles, her tongue taps
messages behind his earlobe
while they watch Cocteau's Orphée
being driven. She imagines
the word love like satin
sheets folded away in a drawer,
lets him weigh her breasts
in his hands at night.
She wants to be lost
and return with this
boy she knows she can
name years from now
without feeling.

2.
He drives too fast to Old Sweden-
bourg Road—backs into a bed
of multiflora rose to park, and she thinks
This is life, and laughs—in love with her own
tenderness, his clumsiness with her
buttonholes and hooks.   As if in a dream
his hand has grown into her thighs. It seems
to her that somewhere else, not here,
he's tasting a young girl's
juice. But when he lurches into her,
she bites down hard on that girl's cry.
She sees her own face—
a tiny image in his
open eyes, and she thinks death
might last forever.

The Expanse Between Porch and Sky

A boy straddles farm dirt and freedom, leans
against his shovel, dreaming past dust to sky-
scrapers which signal their smooth-faced promises.

Evenings he weaves star necklaces for his girl.
She searches for peaches' warm fur in his jeans;
his head falls back, throat exposed. He whispers

to an open night, "Baby, baby," reaches for his girl
as if she's a path winding somewhere past dust
to a shade of blue that has nothing to do with prairies

or pig farms. At home he dreams tornados—
five, writhing in a row on the horizon—dreams
he shouts to warn family, but nobody heeds.

They grin and nod, lift Coke bottles like Stygian
sacraments on the front porch: a façade clouded
with their complacency. He wakes hungry

to hold his girl against twister nights, to ride
the ozone of their undulant flights, risk
the vortex that would sail them both past dust

to highways that fissure porch and sky, to palm
peach blossoms in their own time's pleasure—
thirty dollars in their pockets, a tankful of gas:
the centrifugal yearning of young creatures.

In the Heart of Illinois State Fair

Twilight's cover urged me
to talk back to the ring-toss carney.
He knew the odds well—
the table set with erect
rough boards that plastic rings
could barely encompass:
he showed me
again and again
that north south pumping
of ring over board.

I thought I understood
how man considers woman,
how she can bask in the fireglow
of a strange man's eyes
and remain an option within
her own will. From this smug
safety, I laughed and said
"Get lost."

Then they all stood, two rows
of dirt-lined righteous anger,
stood oily and tall in their wooden cages,
shouting, "Rip you in half,
bitch, come on," and I ran,
knowing I belonged to the world.

Reputation

after "Prostitute with Dog and Tulips,"
by Anne Howeson

In the glossy deep-pink room, the white
curtains open, you read a woman's book
underlined at the good parts; an unseen
chair keeps you off the floor.

Outside the window, critics
gather—a man in a trench coat, of course,
and two who write you love sonnets
with their tallest finger. Others are laughing
at some *carpe femina* joke.

Inside three pink tulips overlook
the window commotion, waiting
for the hour they pick to toss down petals
and rise like a smaller version of a man's
fist against the brush-stroked heat of this room.

The crowd of men bides your time,
asking each other the way to your door, rifling
the edges of fat rolls of family-man
bills in their pockets. One presses
his face against the glass as if
the open curtains were your thighs.

After all, they're wide open, the men say,
she could close herself in darkness,
hide behind shades. Look, the dog
she holds by the collar is smaller than we are;
it can mean us no harm.

None find your bell.
They shuffle, speak loud about breaking
a new doorway. Their eyebrows agree
you'll think it a gift, something to cause you
to lay down the book, to wear the dog's collar.

Siamese Twins in Love

A lifetime mirrored: Chang and Eng,
marked into filling the same
space in a freeze-frame of tours
lined with round-eyed faces. You face
the cameras in painful twists,
no smiles. Your eyes,
wild with separate desires
in youth, have opaqued into stoic
reflections. You move as one beast—
even when you marry, buy American
homes only blocks apart, stretch the mirror
until edges bevel into two worlds
you give each other: three-days altered
with each wife, sisters who must
have shared everything.

Nothing can stop us from thinking
of how a wife must straddle
the mirror you make, how one
pair of hips twists to meet her.
And you and you always
smell his same rank sweat
as it laps your skin, his heat
yours, an endless touch
spreading from joined breastbone
to the twinned tightening of nipples,
their points rising like small worms
fattened on lust for hot rain.
Such intimate brotherly love endures
conditional tense. You love to watch
his eyes that mirror yours roll back
as your backs arch, and you undulate
again into beast, want to lay
your tongue down his identical throat.

Chang's Wife Takes to Gin

The choreographed touch of years
has deformed our nights;
we no longer imagine
the luxury of an unheard whisper,
fantasy of a satin night alone.

Tabloids burn with our stories:
two sisters, two brothers, four pairs
of eyes, four wet mouths. Impatient, I watch
twisting bodies that readers only dream,
eyelids like moviehouse screens.

        I perform a circus act,
racing inside a golden ring, sell
tickets to the execution of my dreams,
and my ears leap to money's
crinkle as if it were a cracked whip.

        Once I loved a man
for his eyes, a black maze
like a fingerprint. But I follow a beast
who hides from my false sunlight,
who laps the poison I give to myself.
Knowing I wrote this act, I open
my mouth and hear my sister's
voice scream its brief pleasures.

Day Breaks Her Window

The rain will not leave. Paralyzed
in the air; on the ground,
it shines and wants to slither. I see
the rose of my hands, folded, glistening,
while houses and trees are awash
from rain's gray rags. The world
has taken a step back

into watered shadows. I would call out,
but my lungs splash against my ribs.
A lamp always burns somewhere.
Even when light drips gray, I smell
its defaulted bright perfume.

Nightfall Brushes Her Hair

In the dusk of my heart there are
no safe places. Thin-skinned
winged emotions flap their blind
interior paths and sometimes scream
just to let themselves know where
they are. That they are.

My heart's landscape
has no corners in which
to be painted, only chambers
with doors that won't stay shut.
I find no rest. Heart
dances its transient squeeze
and red-coats its walls in
velvet, the faithful panting
of a loyal pet that would give
its life, that will give no recourse.

This heart, in heat, races
ahead, while I haven't heard
the gun. A woman thing, some
say. Spares me the trouble
of climbing the belfry,
clanging the bell.

Chang Runs Away From Home

Bones like a tuning fork begin to hum

O Flesh of my Flesh

What is the sound of half a heart beating

A plantain peels, reveals its solitary bone

Mind and body, splitting

Meat roasted so long it falls from the bone

Green bamboo bows into two equal halves

East is East

To bow forward from the waist

The last man left on the interior planet

Theatre of the mind, eyelids as screen, closed to the public

White butterflies of exquisite discontent

The dream of a singular peach blossom

Tree floats away on silken air

Eng Writes to Chang

begs him to return. In a blue-edged note
slipped into Chang's pocket, Eng presents

his argument, buried as deep in habit
and the silence of customary flesh as

their petrified shoulderblades. The obvious
spans this jeopardy, a carp-filled pool Eng leaps,

four-legged as a stag. Beyond bonds'
silence, the stoic faces of a people, a silken

wish of dancing or dreaming alone
in a white room, Eng reaches for words

that turn into a peach blossom when
he holds them—so—in his anxious palm.

Blood's Inkwell: Eng Writes Chang's Eulogy

*Siamese twin Eng lived in horror for four hours longer
after his brother Chang, a heavy drinker, died.*

Eng still wears the bruises
on his soul from last year's
discussions of the fine arts—
wine and spirits. On top, Chang
pummels him into silence.
Eng's arm still whines from the pain
of dragging his drunken imago
from bedroom to bath, unzipping,
gently holding up the helpless head
of his brother's sex so the urine smell
wouldn't follow them back to bed,
pungent as a wife's accusations.

Chang's giddy blood chases its sodden tail
from the liver's minefield through Eng's
tell-tale heart. The mirror fragments
to shards, the sharpest of which is drawn
across Eng's neck until he sings
sotto voce, tendons tight as strings
of a violin in the grasp of a stage-
fearful musician. Poe never told
this story: the dead body cell-stitched
to your own, the other grave you were
born to. Chang smiles, slowly turns
the color of his pillow.
Eng watches his own reflection
glaze in Chang's dark eye like breath
on a cold window. One of the climbers
falls through an ice passage; the other
slips after him, cursing the fleshy cord.

The Gypsy Teaches Her Grandchild Wolfen Ways

All tongues tell their monsters, shapes
that shift from human to hell   under bridges
and beds: woman crouches to carnivore
or man twists to fiend. They leave howls
inside you forever.

But werewolf's a charmer, mouth full
of bone-glint, handsome
as a polished gun   all sass and Satan.
Stars flicker in wolfen smiles like light
off a knife blade   hard
under soft lips.

Werewolf chases
the red ride in your heart   beams
radar eyes to track blood's hot
dance. You turn   wolf's on you—
wants you for your organs   you,
Fool, who brings kibble and collar.

Sometimes in blue moon's night
werewolf sulks mourns lonely in self's
heartless shadow.   For a moment
werewolf trades murder's sweet drink
for a soul   silver voice to warn you
with cries like rabbits sobbing before death.
Now you think, *I can bewitch the beast*,
grasp handfuls of fur, pull wolf through you
as if your heart's a hoop.
Turn again, child;
pray the gleam shines from faith not fang.

Barcelona in Love

Tonight *Las Ramblas* is paved with dark eyes,
street vendors *hablando*, the screams of parrots
like bright knives slash the rain-glutted flowers,
clouds of petals swirl. When I place the olive
in your tongue's sly fork, my fingers warm to breath
as fired as picador's bloodlust as he turns to stone

some black beast, roses thrown like velvet stones.
Soft strata—lid, lashes, chocolate—horizons your eyes,
a selfish path I climb, raised not to fall, to waste breath,
cut my throat on your trousers' crease. Our slow dance parrots
the city's wine-dark nights, wharf rats in corners, an olive's
heart-stone hidden in green satin flesh. Salt-sense flowers

on the tongue like lovers' sweat. You brought flowers
like a night's payment, Moroccan hashish to stone
our senses into a tapestry of peach against olive
skin, velvets that clash, that blend, guarded by eyes
that refuse to make this moment vision. Our parrot-
bright stares access the opponent, rhythm of breath

calculates desires. The sweet venom of your breath
amuses me almost as much as the show-off flowers
you idly tap, fingers fluttering like wings of parrots
excited by a passing shadow. You are one more stone
skipping across love's lake. If your soul were gossamer, my eyes
would etch you designs that would make your olive

skin pale, but you believe your own lies: the olives
I slip through your lips you imagine, in one breath,
pay your toll, in the next, enamour me. In your eyes,
Yanqui women swoon for Latin romancing, flowers,
and vowel-honeyed words. Let me tell you of stone,
my peacock, of curious yellow, of desire that merely parrots

the love you think you are making. *Las Ramblas'* parrots
sway in cages, practicing scarlet hues against moss-olive
buildings that stand empty, quiet in their own stone
surety. Here's where I begin; take a granite breath.
Let my eyes melt chocolate, my tongue talk flowers
back at you. Isn't it romantic? The game shines your eyes,

while the parrots scream you warning in every breath.
They know this olive will choke you; forgotten flowers
tumble to stone. Suave tones die in lust's sensible eyes.

Naked in the Demimonde

The naked man seeks clothing for protection.
—Thomas Carlyle

He touches her throat   with taut intent,
not like the old days   of dances, wet kisses,
the days when he'd polish   her breasts with his palms.
She wears a shirt   woven tightly
of yellow hair,   the heavy threads
crossing over, under   until she can't
remember their source,   her memories a snake
asleep in her belly.   Dark blue blossoms,
her jewelry, the size   and shape of fingertips
around her neck,   here on her arm.
A slap of rose   on one silk cheek,
and eyes as black   as a leather belt—
she's the shadow queen   of the empty scream
and the demimonde code   of thick makeup and lies,
clenched into a figure   of his fist and fears.
She lies awake listening   alone until
she hears his car   at the nightmare hour,
coming home from places   he hides in his eyes.
He swings his body   over hers like a shroud
and she closes her eyelids   to his lost language,
crosses her arms,   close to bare breasts.

44

Folded

Stunned, she's alone
with the uselessness of hands,
everything around
shining wet and poignant
as a single drop of dew
on a very pink rose.
The clock says tock so slowly—
a command in dead language
she can't speak.
Hands fill her lap,
a shell collection
ridged and worn,
not part of the body,
not part of the confusion
of bone and vein.
Pale spiders wait
to make or unmake
the webs they weave.
They don't care which.

And Also See

Winter clings stubborn as 11 p.m.
in a second-shift dead-end job.
On Highway 150 home, my car
slushes through an inch of late snow,
while the moon beams its half-hearted spotlight,
full of lies and promises on this time-
slowed ghost road, trees slipping past,
their limbs raised in surprise: *This is your life?*

Halfway through a heartbeat, a deer
runs sudden next to my car,
runs hard, wearing its velvet mask,
antlers determined and framed
in my passenger window,
runs with no sign of startle,
next to—not away from—the road,
not flat-out racing but leaping
undulant, skimming the ground,
tossing snow like jet vapors behind,

runs with joy; I know
I invent this—but it invents
me in return: a deer appears
from darkness, stays with me
long enough to spin moonlight to gold
and then
            takes the hill
by the road in three bounds,
leaps the futile fence at the top.

Nightmoves

We stretch out, lean back
on a tenement stoop
under a night sky full
of our only diamonds.
Two friends from the bright days
of tight sweaters and tight dreams
that have since lost their shapes,
we watch the street slide by,
nightmoves of cars, drunks
and audacious dogs,
look for a sign from the stars,
a cosmic lottery.

The sky stretches out
on its back—stretches out
down the universe
and does not contemplate
two friends.
Constellations twist
like gears in the sky
A star falls like a spark.
We imagine the sky
moves around us tonight,
that the brightest star
pivots.

Stay on the Planet

I swear there is no death
that can sift you, the quiet
white motes of you, into oblivion.
Wherever you look, there are only
more changes.
                The blue day plumps
into eggplant night; colors drip
from errant paintbrushed clouds
until the final chords of Deep Purple
close the eyes of half a world. How many
of us sleep at any moment? Less than all.

A bird skeleton in the garden becomes a paned
doorway to the iris's sheer ballet. You
have only seconds to read this—
the rest of your life. All your hard-
wood trees may dissolve, all the cardinals
drop like blood to the open green arms of backyards,
friends fade away, smiling. But always
in this any-moment, you can hear the ocean
sigh its ignorance of time, toss waves
to sand casual as pitched cards
or agents, carrying in their watery pockets
small travelers—motes, atoms,
ingredients of the planetary vichyssoise—
scooping back into the ocean's salty lap
spices of another pale creature's concoction.

Scan your jagged horizons. They won't stop
at any blade's edge that you can name.
Return to the wilderness, the shoreline
again and again. Bring balloons
full of your sighs, your terrible dreams,
and let the colors drift past sunsets, past
all life's stubborn elements that float,
spring, fly, orbit, decompose, reform—
all that you are, rafting through the relentless
notions of the senses—beautiful, strong,
and careless of any happy ending.

Ascent to Mountaintop, No Chariot

Sonaguerita, Honduras

You strap your clothes on back
and climb onto the spine of a horse or mule
     that has never been someone's pet
     that won't care how much you cluck
     to woo it out of nettles
     nor how much mountain air you suck
     making kisses to hurry it
     past a mere sheer drop.
And when you see yourself halfway
to heaven, halfway into a two hour ride,
and the trail has narrowed into a clay snake
and the side of the mountain nearest
the very frayed cinch that pends your saddle
within the clouds is the steepest drop
your escaping heart has never dreamed of,
don't imagine you can say, like T.S. Eliot
talking to cats: *O horse! O mule!*
do be careful at this point. Like lesser angels
they remain nameless. They have no options
to give you except to cling to this hairy,
thin-flanked belief, to bow forward when heaven's path
tilts steep as the ladder in a dream, and when you get all
the way up, to remember it's not the last ride.

I Stroke Death by the Eight-Foot Jesus

that they ask me to paint on the village church
wall. The good shepherd, lamb, of course,
on his arm—I paint him dark and sweet
as endless sleep—a Mona Lisa-tease
smile and eyes that look everywhere
in surprise. The villagers watch, hanging
like grapes in the windows, swelling
through doorways onto the cement floor,
whispering *What does it mean?* I can't tell
them the lifespan of eight-foot dreams,
brush in more Honduran mountains behind
giant Jesus, and the path villagers struggle
up then down wriggles like a snake under his feet.

It's said he followed a twisted path;
I imagine he stopped
at the pinnacle of some mountain,
like the one we stand on, where the tallest
palm tree, eager as a priest, points out our descent.
He must have seen in the heavens how death slides
by on ebony wings through the complacent air, circling
what must die. He must have seen his fate, etched
in a midnight feather, known whose pale hand,
like that in a Michelangelo dream, loosed the darkness
that casts living souls into shadows.

                             I dip the brush in paint
the color of Jesus' eyes and add the last small strokes
in the mural's sky, the strokes that form the vulture flight,
cante jondo, the perpetual song of bones pale
with mourning's ancient light, notes only humans
can hear or intone. I add the scavenger close enough
to Jesus' shoulder to be his father's hand. The church
is quiet; a scorpion crawls from under stained boards.

The Ceiba Tree

La Ceiba, Honduras

His too-small shirt might have been
red and white once.
Orphan of God
maybe six years old
lies on the sidewalk, his face
pillowed by cement. He wears
only the shirt. I can't
wake him. Drugs, someone
whispers, in a country
where the word must be
whispered. I hide
lempiras and peppermints
behind the boy's head and later
dream of executions in the streets.

The city was named for the tree that grows
along the northern edge, past the fetid canal
that snakes by the poorest shanties. They loom
from the mud like herons, poised over the small
creatures at their feet. The roots lift themselves
out of the earth, far above the common people,
like the massive thighs of the old white gods
on horseback. The ceibas cover good fields
in shadows; the roots sinuate between houses of friends.
The trees are protected by law, people say, but the children aren't
forbidden to climb and play in the roots. *Mira*, how they arch
above the earth like the beams of Eternal Virgin Cathedral.

Gracias al Señor for our blessings
Gracias al Señor for the Americans who build schools we can sleep in
Gracias that the rats have not come to our cornfields
Gracias al Señor that we have food tonight to give to the Americans
Nuestro Señor, watch over Eduardo, missing son

No safe water, but you can buy
Coca-Cola at any bar or closet-
like store. Needing to see the sights,
five of us go out for Cokes
tonight, scrubbed and pink

as babies. As we sit in the bar
and subtly gawk, a pickup truck loaded
with uniformed men pulls up outside.

I can't remember colors having been so vivid
             at night, nor the smell of wild roses so heady
as when time was stunned by a machine gun
             aimed at every tiny hole in my eyelet blouse.
Pale flesh, bright new clothes make us issues,
and our passports are in the hotel. Machinegunfire
words sizzle from one soldier's mouth
and I'm the only gringa who speaks Spanish.

                   Excuse me; they don't speak Spanish.
Tell the men to put their hands on their heads!
                   Do it. They're going to frisk you.
Bueno. Tell them to sit down and don't go anywhere.

They arrested a Honduran with a gun down his pants.
Later I thought I could've
had a bomb in my purse, I could've
had a gun. They never checked
the two women, just nailed us
into silence with the machinegun's
stiffness, its waivering eye.

No one knows where the trees came from
or how long they'll live. The last night in Honduras,
I walk the city's edge, surrounded by children
browner than the soil of stripped mountains, children
who plead for coins, for gum, for remembrance.
                             At the edge,

the ceiba tree groans out of the earth, twenty hardened feet up
of roots exposed to the triviality of air. The shanties
settle into the dust. Somewhere a siren screams, a gun fires,
and men are laughing. While across the canal
the city streets twist into twilight like shadows
of tortured people.

Authority

Faded travel posters snicker,
you are going Nowhere. For two hours
we sit in the Roatan airport, shifting
our buttocks on stern wooden benches
in a room long and low like a coffin.
Shoulder to shoulder we line the walls,
our sunglasses like blindfolds in this glaring country.
We wait for authority's permission to rise.

Honduran authority moves slowly. It yawns
and takes siestas. It walks through the room
in shiny boots, shirt half undone, and it likes
to snort and look disdainful enough not to need
the gray-barrelled pistol stroking its flank. Authority
has a pungent stink and sleeps wherever it wants to.

In La Ceiba we stand for three hours
in a cattle-car room, wire-fencing
twelve feet high. Small children are corralled
helpless in hips and crotches. We wait;
authority will not meet our eyes. It empties
our bags, fingers it all with staged disinterest.

        Leaving Honduras we will save
something for authority. Boxes of soap
given to guards as gifts slip us through the gates.
Our bags aren't plundered.

Intentions of Shade

Honduran heat comes from an old god's
belly—Chacmol—who never thought
of baptism by any water
other than sweat from your body,
sacrificial drops, like life
left somewhere
on a mountain's green altar.
You dream of November prairie winds,
of your naked body pinked by snowdrifts,
of an ice shard, your missing link.

The villagers are uncomfortable
with your discomfort.
Your smile has shriveled at the edges.
Shy, they bring you Cokes,
lukewarm from standing
in the clay store's shade. Here the law
of quenching your ungodly heat is to roll
yourself and the empties back up the mountain,
up its steep red slant past pointed sunrays
to the store with Coke beading out of your pores,
gods and small children laughing.

The villagers wait in the wizened shadow
of a lemon tree for you to finish.
They want to spare you the worst,
walk the mountain for you,
their eyes darker than cloudy nights.
A Coke, you've heard, costs a week's wages.
Elba and Hilda lift like small birds from the shade,
reach for your task. They become taller,
bolder than red hills; their dark bodies
seeming to rise like shadows of late afternoon's
trees, laying hands on the land's fever.

The Diarrhea Brochure

      I tell them nothing
they want to hear: spend more time breaking your back
over low clay ovens to boil water, drink seven glasses
of warm, boiled water a day, take the same to your husband
who has no canteen, who is hanging off the mountain
by a rope to work fields.

      You must dig a latrine
downhill in the jungle, make sure the family all use it—
no doubt because of the water you must drink—

      and you must keep
your animals out of the hut, even when it's cold and wet
and their bodies are warmer than yours. Even when it's hot,
and the breeze of an open door would save you. I hold
up pictures that go with my sterile story, squares
of cardboard showing pigs running rampant, children shitting
on the floor, prepping their hands in it like diabolical doctors.

      I speak of invisible monsters
swimming indolent circles in water they drink, how the favored
pig bundles bugs into clay huts like a guerrilla, how this mission
passes to their smiling infants who pat the visible and invisible
with hands already the color of earth.

Honduran fathers have no investment
in my domestics, and the mothers' eyes are curtained,
a third eyelid to protect from Western notions. I speak
marigolds' yellow language, here, on a mountain where bright
hibiscus shout from the mud, rampant down red hillsides.

Teaching Chinese Checkers in Central America

The speechless board, the mint-
sized magnet pieces won't confess
their secrets in Honduran farmers'
tongue. The men sit beyond
our compound on rough benches holding
brown babies fed, dressed, with thick
black baby-hair watered and combed.
Their women cook. I am not
cooking. I am not working
on the mural in the church. But I may be
about to do some unknown American
task they risk rudeness to interrupt.
Their backs are stiff with listening: *Will you?*

Eduardo, who asks, cannot contain his joy. His smile
spreads the gameboard wide on the bench.
The sunlight scatters sparkles on white squares
of his teeth, his work-scarred fingers herd
colored checkers pieces to corners, like with like.
The men gesture to older children: come
take the babies out of their laps. Then their warm
breath brushes the back of my neck. If I turn,
that shy air would cool quickly, lean back on the fence,
ignore explanations of move and jump.
I hear the question of history over possibility:
How can a woman know the game?

How Eduardo, Thirteen-Year-Old
Head of Household, Spends His Summer

First his long look
over the sharp-faced
mountain's edge,
then he ties the rope
to a believable palm
and lowers himself
to the next tiny shelf.
Small spaces on which
to grow corn lie
flattened like frightened
rabbits' ears
against all the edges
he might fall from—
a fall not of floating
but of crashing, rolling,
breaking over and over,
the mountain ignorant
of how to catch him.

His machete licks weeds,
slits the soil
until it lies receptive
to rain and seed.
He climbs down farther
checking his future
footprints for the green viper,
tomogaso verde,
whose fangs would puncture
the fine fabric
of his dreams. Without
water, he works, without
amigos nearby, only the sun's
indolent crackling above him.
His mother wants him to go back to school.
But he'd never let her work the mountain.

Songbird: The Arribatamiento

In the front of the clay church a mural
of the second coming collapses houses,
tortures sinners to their knees, while overhead
the tiny white forms of primitive Christians fly
with arms raised like superman into the heavens.
The caption in black between the good and the goners
reads *Arribatamiento*, the lifting up of the church.

More uplifting than promise, a guitar begins
a honeyed phrase, opens the throats of the village.
When the people sing, you first hear their harmony,
settled as the mountains and sure among family.
But something is coming
up though their firm notes, through
their seated voices. A song soars up
like a bird of paradise from the jungle,
sleek and full of color, with a long dipping
tail that slips melody to plunge, clarion
at the end of a phrase.

The Honduran women smile and nod,
whisper, *Nora*, and point to her with their chins.
The songbird's a child, ten years old, they say,
and she's held to the music by her skyward smile,
her throat's willingness to be exposed. This voice
queens itself over the guitar and violin, pulls
the villagers across notes like stepping stones,
suspends us for a time in a place between riot
and rapture, more real than all the mural's blood
and black marks. Like a guitar strummed sweet
in the thick hands of a farmer, her voice forgets
its place and sings the rough angels silent.

News to You
—for the geographically indifferent

Yesterday you knew the world was flat
       "Earthquake in Salvador kills hundreds"
Yesterday you knew the count was only 400:
Hardly more than a Schwarzenegger movie
        The living sleep by fires in the streets
It's winter on this side of the flat earth
with two sides to our Western flats:
the media's calm drone, your opinion in the bar
Flat as Texas
Flat as a fritter
So flat you can rollerblade in Speedos, easy,
or drive one of your three cars, leisurely,
going nowhere on play money or plastic
For flat worlders, Salvador is beyond
the vanishing point,
There but not there

You could drive that hog to Salvador
in four days, if you didn't
have better things to do.
But if you went, in designer camo,
surely the body count would be lower

Not your fault that Salvador has no
good hotels, steel-reinforced huts,
a national emergency power source,
a plan   And how many
people live in Salvador, anyway?
Weren't they wiped out
in some domestic conflict?
Didn't we send them help back then?

Thin Air Is Where

The next frontier hovers like a trauma
That you can't wait to read in the news:
The unsolvable solved, Jimmy Hoffa floats
Like a serene Buddha, chanting, *What the*
Hell; it's my karma. Thin air squats
At the edge of reality's pious horizon,
Heavy as a mountain, the last bastion
For the great conspiracies. Then thin
Air's thick shell hardens ennui
Into speculation's horny perversions:
Who puppeteered Lee Harvey Oswald,
James Earl Ray, the aliens in Area 51?
What obscure nursing home cradles
Elvis, Evita, Elijah, and Lennon?

Flesh-bound mortals can't breathe thin air,
Must wait outside, faces pressed
Against its milky shell as if it were
A breast or a gummy peep-show window. Once
You vanish into thin air, you won't likely
Be winked at again. From the mists of *what if*,
You'll enjoy *Twilight Zone*'s game
Prolonged to the tune of *Jeopardy* and
The faint whimpers of your loved ones.

Pity those who return from thin air,
Always revised: brain-damage, memory-
Loss, a mission to speak the So-Called
Truth. And when those thin-
Air survivors die, their visions hiss
Out-of-body into the breathlessness
Beloved of gods and small children.

When the Fat Lady Sings

you think of plump bonbons filled
    with pliant surprise
        like cream to lick or caramel, chewy
           enough to stick
with you longer than anything fluffy
    ever would and
        when you hear her take that high
           note that note that
shakes the plexiglass oversized shower
    you are in church
        in the back in the dark while the giant
           pipes of an organ
the size of a cathedral wall shake your
    bones those puny strings
        that whine and shiver while voice swoops
           to bass like a pink-sequined
trapeze artist sworn to fling loose
    of the bar and soar
        into the music of the spheres all the spheres
           of the fat lady tremble
from this sound that erupts from her throat
    this call beyond flesh
        o woman something solid as earth as
           liquid as its center

Sideways Through the Looking Glass

Baring her teeth, the Fat Lady stacks chins like scallops.
Dressed in red for her devotees, she sweats Max Factor
puddles under the Shirley Temple wig. Even the hairs
of her moustache are monumental, stouter than wisps

of little women who pay to stare at what she has built
with flesh. The ladies cringe, float home feeling lighter
than willow branches stroking the ground, whichever
way the wind blows them. Men ogle her, dream fat,

fantasize huge Sex, breasts' and belly's firm mountains
yielding to earthquake orgasms: her only speed,
grateful waterbed of their kinked desire. Six hundred
and fifty-three pounds play hide-and-seek with her

aching feet, her vulva—a round word for something
gone flat as the world once was, for all she knows.
When the congregation bows out, she waits for Ernie
to close stage curtains at her workday's end. He'll heave her

out of her chair, joke about massive breasts burying,
smothering him in love. Hafta be a big man for a woman
like me, she slow-trills in bass. What if you disappear?
He always does; she's deserted, ghost ship, his parting slap

at her rump. She'll limp slowly, all wheeze and sway
like the carnival's Moonwalk tent, back to her trailer—
her ruffled pink curtains and plum satin sheets—to hide
with cigar-sized nipples, an empty pop bottle's pleasure.

I Tell Myself Yellow

Holding something tenuous in my
clumsy hands, your heart, for example,
I'm afraid
of the weight of it, its fine shine
like gold-bordered china I end up
breaking: I step on the shards
for the rest of my life—
reminders of yellow lines I cross
into oncoming traffic,
asleep at my own wheel.

I tell myself yellow
is for caution, for being
alert, for not being run over by
you, for example. Then I think
of when we make love, how lines
vanish from all roads. We weave
shoulder to shoulder as in a dream
where the driver disappears and
you surrender to the ride.

So often lately I want to write you
down—the warm-cloves smell of you,
the sweet hollows my hands dip into
sliding down your hips—something I know
I could keep. But yellow contracts my hands
to hammers—the claws, a hawk's.
I wake myself in midfall, shivering
from the speed of it.

Our Bodies Speak Their Lines

to my sons

Pieces of you disappear. I know
when next I look, something else
will vanish. Your baby fat melts
from curves of stumbles and bounce
into the hard and slick sculpturing
of male animal. Even your young glance
is lithe with impatience. To make
your breaks, you conjure thousands
of other men parting seas with car keys and cash,
a justice pulled from containers I don't remember
seeing around the house before. Your words
become linear, arrange themselves
in two lines that intersect like a prow.

And I have become more round. Hips
that used to move straight ahead now sway
and, I imagine, favor the left. I'm more
aware of the bowl of my inner sex, its designs
on who I think I am. The curved lines of body
lean slightly downward to earth, like weighted
wheat, the rich-smelling grain certain now of how
to knead sun. What more can I tell you of stars?

My body darkens into solitary fields,
and you transform into your future. I celebrate
the fading of old snapshots, our laughter
over deceitful, new ones. At one time
your soft eyes looked for me
in every daybreak, your hand catching
mine to cross any rough street. But at this
age, your eyes create a deep backdrop
for stars in heavens I can't quite see.
I know when next we look at each other,
something else will have vanished.

Blue Catfish

It is impossible to see the angel unless you first have a notion of it.
—James Hillman

As if the mighty river took
a loyalty oath to shield you
with its body, it floats you deep
and dark as an old family secret,
locks you into the murky depths
where river boats wait their turns
to step down that great water road.

Rivermen swear they've seen
the big one—ten foot long,
pectoral spine like a quarterstaff—
sucking down all manner of garbage
from spillways, a fellow brawler,
lover of stink and the shad-filled slough.

The sins of humans stream past you,
petty grievances of diamond rings and spit,
hate tied in ropes or wire, a tumbling
Frigidaire spectre. Condoms swirl and beckon.
A truck tire whose afterlife can never unfold
in fire nor water waits for the Apocalypse.
A man in overalls, laced into a deadwood
tangle, waves a slow salute. Our various guilt
eddies or sinks in dilatory denial past your flat,
jelly eyes. You chronicle the decades and sift

the muddy bottom without judgment,
gargling the poisons, lipping the death,
unexacting, nature's Cronos, whose pale
blue skin mimics high heaven, rising
from the river darkness like a heavy soul
or salvation.

Acknowledgments

"Tenderest," winner, St. Louis Poetry Center Stanley Hanks Award, *River Styx*

"Dr. StrangeLove," *River Styx* (published as "Frankenfreud")

"Louisiana Ladies' Watermelon Tea—1980," *Feminist Studies*

"Goddess Discord Brings Her New Doll Buggy into My Yard
     When I Don't Want Her There," *Baybury Review*

"Strange Fruit," *The Legendary*

"Our Man Thumb," *Laurel Review*

"Tom Thumb Dreams," "The Expanse Between Porch and Sky," "Rear Window,"
     Spoon River Poetry Review

"One of the Lesser Gods," *Sou'wester*

"Orpheus in Her Stars: The First Time," *The Cape Rock*

"Siamese Twins in Love," "Nightfall Brushes Her Hair," "Day Breaks Her Window,"
     "Chang's Wife Takes to Gin," "Eng Writes to Chang," "Chang Runs Away from
     Home," *Clockwatch Review*

"Blood's Inkwell: Eng Writes Chang's Eulogy," "The Gypsy Teaches Her
     Grandchild Wolfen Ways," "When the Fat Lady Sings," *Freaks: Poems*

"Naked in the Demimonde," *Nebraska Review*

"Folded," *Lullwater Review*

"And Also See," "In the Heart of Illinois State Fair," *Cuivre River Anthology*

"Nightmoves," *Beloit Poetry Journal*

"Stay on the Planet," "Thin Air Is Where," "News to You," "Family History,"
     Lunarosity

"Ascent to Mountaintop, No Chariot," *St. Louis Post-Dispatch*

"I Stroke Death by the Eight-Foot Jesus, "Teaching Chinese Checkers in Central
     America," *Pikestaff*

"The Ceiba Tree," "Five Deceits of the Hand," *Rhino*

"Authority," "The Diarrhea Brochure," "How Eduardo, Thirteen-Year-Old Head
     of Household, Spends His Summer," *Uncommon Ground: Poems*

"Intentions of Shade," *Analecta*

"Songbird: The Arribatamiento," *Farmer's Market*

"Sideways Through the Looking Glass," *Illinois Review*

"I Tell Myself Yellow," *Whetstone*

"Our Bodies Speak Their Lines," *Negative Capability*

"Blue Catfish," *Down to the Dark River: Poems About the Mississippi River*

CPSIA information can be obtained
at www.ICGtesting.com
Printed in the USA
LVHW091345300321
682964LV00026B/372